CCSS Genre Fiction

W9-AXP-418

Essential Question
Where can your imagination take you?

A Fantastic Day!

by Clara Strongfoot
illustrated by Brian Dumm

Chapter 1
Don't Cry Over Spilled Milk

Ramon got home from school, washed his hands, and sat down at the kitchen counter. His mom put a glass of milk and two fresh oatmeal raisin cookies in front of him.

Ramon gazed at the cookies. "They look like two big eyes staring back at me!" he thought. Ramon had a great imagination.

"Thanks, Mom!" said Ramon. Oatmeal cookies were his favorite snack.

"You're very welcome," said Mom with a smile. "I'm going to finish vacuuming the living room now. Grandma is coming for dinner tonight. After that, we need to clean up your room."

"Let me know when you're ready for help," said Ramon. He noticed a big sponge on the kitchen sink. "Wow! That sponge looks just like a cloud," he thought.

Ramon heard Mom turn on the vacuum cleaner. "That humming noise sounds just like an airplane flying over the house," he thought.

Ramon was daydreaming about airplanes when he reached for a cookie. Whoops! His hand knocked over the glass of milk, spilling it into his plate. That was when Ramon's imagination really took over!

Suddenly, a river of milk began to create a lake. The cookies were two islands floating in the middle. Ramon looked up and saw two noisy airplanes flying overhead. His eyes grew wide as they swooped down. Each plane scooped up one of the islands.

"Wow!" he thought. "I have airplanes in my kitchen!" Then the planes took off.

Now Ramon saw a big, fluffy cloud floating down from the sky. "The cloud is touching the lake and soaking it up," thought Ramon excitedly. "It looks like the cloud is taking a long drink!"

The cloud floated away, and the lake and islands were gone. "That was so cool!" Ramon said aloud.

The vacuum cleaner stopped humming, and Mom came back into the kitchen. She wiped a cookie crumb off Ramon's cheek with a napkin. "Let's clean up your room now, dear," she said.

"Okay, Mom, I'm ready," said Ramon.

Chapter 2

Getting the Job Done

Ramon followed Mom into his bedroom. There were toys, blocks, clothes, and books all over the floor. His bed wasn't made, and the blankets were in a tangle.

Ramon wrinkled his nose and looked at Mom. "I know—it's a big mess!" he admitted.

Mom laughed and said, "We've got plenty of work to do! Let's get going."

Just as Ramon and Mom got started, the phone rang. "I'll see who that is," said Mom, "but you can keep working."

When Mom walked out, Ramon's imagination took over again. Now he saw his toys come to life!

"My robots and animals are helping me clean," thought Ramon. "We make a great team!"

Even Ramon's books were doing their part. They inched their way over to the bookcase and climbed onto the shelf.

"Look at my helpful bookworms!" he thought. "They are crawling to the right spot. Cleaning up isn't that hard when you're part of a team."

Seconds later, a tornado whirled through the open window. "Look at this twister spin and swirl!" said Ramon. First, it blew all the dirty clothes into the hamper. Then it blew over the bed and untangled the blankets.

"Can a tornado fix the sheets?" asked Ramon. "You bet it can!"

When Mom came back, she saw a clean and tidy room. "Good work, Ramon!" she exclaimed. "Grandma will be here soon. Let's get dinner ready."

Chapter 3
Sweet Dreams

Mom made Ramon's favorite meal—macaroni and cheese. Over dinner, Ramon told Grandma all about the airplanes, the islands, the clouds, and the lake.

"You have quite an imagination!" laughed Grandma. "I think you probably got that from me!"

Then Ramon described how his toys and books came to life and helped him clean his room. He was about to mention the tornado, but it was time for bed.

Ramon put on his pajamas and brushed his teeth. Then Grandma tucked him in, and together they read a story.

When they finished the book, Grandma turned off the light and said, "Sleep tight, my dear."

"But I'm not sleepy, Grandma," Ramon complained.

"Try counting sheep," Grandma suggested. She gave him a kiss.

"Okay, Grandma, I'll try," said Ramon.

Ramon pictured sheep jumping over a fence. He started counting, "One...two... three...." But then he stopped. "Sheep are so boring," he thought. That was when Ramon's imagination took over again!

The moonlight became a dazzling, sunlit ocean. Ramon saw a pod of dolphins swim through his bedroom window. They leapt joyfully all around his room. Ramon chose the largest dolphin and climbed onto its back. Now he was leaping over ocean waves with all of his dolphin friends.

"This is as much fun as an amusement park ride!" thought Ramon. "I'm pretty good at riding dolphins!"

The dolphins took Ramon to a sandy beach with rolling waves. It was perfect for surfing.

"Whee! Look at me!" Ramon thought. "Now I'm a surfer!"

But soon, Ramon started feeling drowsy. His eyelids got heavy. It was getting hard to keep his balance.

He found a sandy beach and curled up to rest. "Even surfers have to nap," he thought. The sun warmed his face, and soon he was fast asleep.

Respond to Reading

Summarize

Use important details to summarize *A Fantastic Day!*

Character	Clue	Point of View

Text Evidence

1. How do you know *A Fantastic Day!* is fiction? Genre

2. What is Ramon's point of view about the spilled milk? Include details from the story. Point of View

3. What are the cookies compared to on page 5? Metaphors

4. Write about Ramon's point of view and his mother's point of view. Use details from the story. Write About Reading

Compare Texts

Now read some poems about where your imagination can take you.

A Butterfly Life

I want to be a butterfly
With wings so light and fair.
Flitter, flutter 'round the yard
Sailing in the air.

On trees I sit and sip the sap,
But flowers I love best.
Colors call, smells and all,
A pretty place to drink and rest.

Circus Day

After a day at the circus
I drew my favorite part.
A burly, roaring lion
Standing on a box.

Next I drew a circle
And held it in the air.
That lion roared and jumped right through
And landed on my desk!

When we went to the circus
I'm glad I watched so well.
Now I'm the lion tamer of
The pictures
in my head!

Make Connections

Where does Ramon's imagination take him? **Essential Question**

How do the story and poems show people using their imaginations? **Text to Text**

Focus on
Literary Elements

Dialogue When characters speak to each other, they use dialogue. Looking at dialogue can help you understand a character's point of view.

What to Look for As you read a story, look for quotation marks: " ". They show when characters are speaking to each other. Look at this example from the story.

"Try counting sheep," Grandma said.

Your Turn

Write a story with characters using dialogue. Have your characters go on an adventure in their imaginations. Use quotation marks around the words each character says.